Empath Survival Guide

A Practical Guide for Highly Sensitive People to Build Connections With Others – A Healing Workbook to Develop Your Emotional Intelligence, Improve Self-Esteem and Self-Confidence

Marc Goossens

Table of Contents

Introduction

Congratulations on purchasing *Empath Survival Guide: A Practical Guide for Highly Sensitive People to Build Connections With Others – A Healing Workbook to Develop Your Emotional Intelligence, Improve Self-Esteem and Self-Confidence* and thank you for doing so.

The following chapters will discuss how empaths, being so sensitive as they are, can adapt to this world where their self-confidence will always be put to the test. This book aims at providing you relevant tips that will help you develop your levels of emotional intelligence and also form a deep connection with those around you without compromising your own needs. My goal is to teach the empaths how they can embrace their qualities and learn to see sensitivity from a completely new perspective.

When you learn to control your highly sensitive nature, coping with the setbacks in life will become way easier than you ever imagined it to be. Empaths have the habit of soaking up all the negative energy around them and this can affect them in quite unhealthy ways if they cannot control their emotional powers. So, are you someone who gets overwhelmed by the emotions of others around you? Then, don't worry, as this book will provide you the answer to all your questions and also introduce you to a new way of living. So, don't let anyone demoralize you by saying that you are too sensitive and know it in your heart that you are special.

There are plenty of books on this subject on the market, thanks again for choosing this one! Every effort was made to ensure it is full of as much useful information as possible; please enjoy!

Chapter 1: Signs That You Are an Empath

Before we dive into the details of this chapter, let me first give you an idea of who an empath really is. Basically, anyone who has the ability to understand and really feel what the other person is feeling is called an empath. Although it might seem to you that probably anyone can understand what someone else is feeling, but you are wrong. There are so many aspects to understand if you want to know what it really means to be a true empath. It is true that expressing empathy is something many of us can do. It is also true that some people are better at it than others. But when you are an empath, you will be able to feel the other person's emotions as if it were your own. And I do not only mean verbally expressed emotions and thoughts but also the things that the other person might find difficult to express.

As an empath, you will be sensitive to a lot of things around you, and your overall energy levels along with your physical wellbeing, can be hugely affected by these things. So, if you are confused about whether you are an empath or not, I have listed some of the common signs shown by empaths.

You Know When Something is 'Off'

Even when a person does not express his/her feelings, an empath can easily sense it. They can tell when a person is suppressing something even before they have told anything to anyone. This trait of empaths is usually something that makes them a good friend. When a person is in need of emotional support, empaths are usually the first ones to notice. But, it also makes life difficult for them because even when they are having a carefree time with friends, a small change in someone else's mood (which is not visible to others) can cause a change in their mood as well. The moment they realize that someone is less than happy, empaths are the first ones to go and make them feel better, and in that process, they absorb all the negative energy from that person.

You Feelings Fluctuate With That of Others

You were having a brilliant day since morning until you met someone on the way to work who was having an awful day. At that moment, you forget all the productive things you have done all day and how happy you were, and you dive into the sorrow of that person. Your emotions start changing their course. You feel angry or sad or whatever emotion the other person is having and all your good vibes are gone just like that. One of the common traits of every empath is that they cannot separate other's emotions from theirs. They get easily affected by someone else's energies.

You Always Experience Emotional Fatigue

Compassion is one of the primary traits displayed by empaths. But the emotional fatigue that comes hand-in-hand with compassion can be quiet threatening for their well-being. Empaths often experience burnouts just because they cannot identify their emotional fatigue while there is still time. Think of it this way – every human experiences fatigue when they are feeling low or any such negative emotion. But an empath has the habit of picking up the emotions of everyone around them and this can become an addictive behavior for them. They cannot stop themselves from absorbing the negative energies others emanate and they take it upon their shoulders to save everyone from their miseries. All that is fine but the problem arises when empaths experience strong emotions of sadness or depression as if they were their own. This leads to a state of constant emotional fatigue.

You Are an Emotional Detective

Empaths are definitely detectives when it comes to identifying emotions. The moment they step foot into a room, they can sense the energy present there. Also, they are extremely good readers of even the smallest changes in body language, facial expression, change in voice, and so on. If someone's body language is not at par with what they are saying, an empath is the first one to notice such changes. Most empaths experience some form of trauma or the other in their childhood years while growing up. They are always told that they are too sensitive for this world and thus not fit to be here. But the same thing also promotes them to have hypervigilance and so they develop an extremely sharp intuition.

In most cases, whatever empaths feel or have to say about a particular situation turns out to be right rather than wrong. They carefully analyze their life experiences and all the trauma and paranoia that they have inculcated since childhood is what promotes them to make accurate judgments. But on the other hand, normal people make decisions based on surface-level interactions alone, and that is why they miss out on several small things that the empaths notice.

Empaths have this amazing ability to immediately catch the undercurrent of an emotion that is going through the other person. Normal people usually miss these signs. For example, a person might be speaking in joy, but in that joy, there may be a tint of jealousy that others miss but an empath will notice it. Whenever there is a dramatic shift about to happen, an empath will immediately feel it. This is also one of the reasons why they can easily tell whether someone is telling the truth or not.

No matter how nice a person is acting, if there is even a shred of contempt beneath that nice behavior, an empath will automatically pick it. If someone has a hidden motive, an empath will be able to sense that too. On the other hand, if the person is truly honest and genuine, an empath can feel that too. They can gain a full insight into the true character of the person. But realizing the truth behind a person can also put them in trouble in certain situations. That is why a riot always acts inside them as to whether or not they should reveal the true image of that person.

Some Other Common Traits

Apart from the ones that we have already discussed, there are so many other traits shared by the empaths, and I am going to list them here for your convenience –

- Empaths really have this habit of finding the victim in every scenario and the underdogs in every place. Empaths are kind of attracted to the people who are going through some kind of suffering or trauma.

- The empaths usually have an excellent skill of imagination, and they have quite creative ideas going on in their mind. Usually, it has been noticed that they possess a lot of talents like dancing, singing, acting, drawing or even writing.

- They are very tidy and minimalist, and if they are living in surroundings that are unkempt or messy, then their flow of energy is hampered.

- Empaths are considered to be compassionate, tolerant and kind, but they also regard narcissism with contempt. In general, they don't prefer staying around those who are egoistic in nature or those who do not think about others at all and prize themselves above everyone else.

- They are usually free spirits; that is, they do not like conforming to the rules someone else sets for them. So, they do not believe in society's constraints and live their life in their own way.

- They are very observant of their surroundings and a very good judge of facial expressions too.

- Other people always seek empaths as their confidante. This is also the reason why they are such easy targets for energy vampires. They are really good at being friends as they are great listeners and they can literally understand your problem like their own. Empaths will go out of their way to help people, but what they do not understand is that sometimes people cannot be helped out of certain situations.

- Empaths usually get tired and want a lot of alone time. This is because they easily get affected by the energies of others.

- They are usually introverts, and the major reason for this is that crowds make them feel overwhelmed and so they prefer conversations on a one-to-one basis rather than a huge party.

- When it comes to intimate relationships, empaths tend to get overwhelmed very easily. This is because empaths do not know how to set healthy boundaries, and their emotions are all over the place. They give too much time to the other person nurturing them that in the end, they do not have any energy left for self-love. And this is also the reason why so many empaths prefer to stay alone rather than be in an intimate relationship.

- When in public, it is quite natural for empaths to feel sudden bouts of overwhelming emotions. And the worst part is that it happens without warning and can happen at any moment.

- Empaths get incapacitated from violent events even if it is happening on TV. They feel such events as if it were happening to them. When they are watching the news, and something is happening to someone thousands of miles away, they feel the pain or loss of that person. Even when it comes to fictional things, empaths feel everything very deeply as if it were real. That is why they do not do well with human tragedy or violence.

- Empaths also have this calming effect on others, which makes them even more special. When someone is present in an empath's presence, he/she automatically feels at peace. That is why empaths are considered to be great healers because they can help you heal from the emotional baggage that you have been carrying around for years.

- Empaths are active listeners. Their listening skills are what helps them understand the situation completely, and that is why other people feel relieved in their presence. No matter how reserved a person is, he/she will be eager to share their deepest sorrows and joys with an empath and it comes naturally to them. There is this unspoken trust and confidence in the air that cannot be explained in words.

- But, an empath can experience extreme highs and lows in their own moods frequently. That is why they have a tendency to show unpredictable behavior at most times. They can be very happy and excited now, but after a few minutes, they might be very angry at something.

- Since empaths often feel that their feelings are not heard, they often come across as needy people.

- Empaths have this intense desire to always seek the truth no matter what, and they are always curious. If they feel that there is something wrong, they will try to reach the bottom of that problem and they will not rest until and unless they find an answer with which they can resonate.

- They are often strong leaders and quiet achievers. This is also because they can understand others so well, and they are very focused. They have qualities of quick thinking and they can easily motivate others too.
- Empaths are very much inclined towards animals and nature in general. They prevent others from doing cruelty on animals as they cannot stand such behavior. They enjoy being amidst the lap of nature or in some mountains away from the busy world.
- They feel the healing properties of water, and that is why they love to be near the sea or the pool. They often love to take hot showers because it feels like the water is cleansing all the negative energies they are carrying.
- Empaths are daydreamers and get usually transported to an entirely different world in their thoughts. They love to doodle.
- They believe in living life fully and are often full of enthusiasm towards it. But this is also the reason why they experience burnout as they tend to waste so much energy in every task.
- Empaths are always seeking meaningful relationships in their lives. Sometimes they also think that self-love is narcissistic and so they deprive themselves of the love that they are ready to give others freely.

Chapter 2: Steps to Follow to Embrace Your Gift as an Empath

You, as an empath, need to understand that this gift that has been bestowed upon you by nature makes you special. If you want to be comfortable with it, you need to learn to accept it. It is true that, at times, you can feel it exhausting to be an empath, both emotionally and physically. And this is also the reason why so many empaths consider their gifts as a burden. But you have to remember that if you want to embrace your gift, then the first step is to feel this burden. After that, you have to learn the best way in which you can look after yourself and stop feeling exhausted at all times.

The process of embracing your gift as an empath will not happen in a day and will require some time, but it is of utmost importance that you embark on this journey. You have to invest your effort and time so that you can come up with the best coping mechanism. Once you are successful in coping with your exhaustion, you will figure out the way in which you can use your gift of empathy to help others. So, here are some ways which you can use in your life to embrace your gift as an empath.

Always Put Yourself First

Empaths have the habit of giving so much of themselves to other people that in the process, they forget to take care of themselves. Empaths often have so much love, and they always want to give it to others but they end up giving it to the wrong people who do not value their love. Instead, these manipulative people suck all the positive energy out from them and leave them exhausted. That is why it is of utmost importance that you always put yourself first and if you do not know how then here are some of the things that you can do –

- Stop thinking that putting yourself first will make others like you less. That is not going to happen. Loving yourself doesn't mean that you will lose your connection with others. People often have the tendency to leave you after judging you whether you like them or not. But those who love you no matter what will be by your side irrespective of your priority list, and these are the people you should be mixing with. When you start putting yourself first, there will be some people who will be confused at first because they are not used to the 'you' who prioritized his/her own needs over others. But that is okay because eventually, they will understand and if they don't then these people don't want you doing well in life. They are the ones who are selfish and toxic.

- If you have this pride within yourself that you are a tireless caregiver, then it is time that you forego that pride. It is true that pride is what gives you a purpose but you also have to learn how you can balance your needs with that of others and only then will you be able to lead a healthy lifestyle. Also, when your energy levels are right, you will have more to give others.

- Stop worrying about missing out on things. This is something empaths often think. They keep checking up on friends and try to know about the latest trends because they think they will be left out if they don't. You need to stop comparing your life to others. Whatever you see on social media is not everything. You see only a part of someone's life, and you don't know what is going on behind the scenes. You will not be able to live your life fully if you keep comparing yourself at all times.

- From childhood years, parents teach their children to put the needs of others first, but that sort of thinking, when practiced over a long period of time, can actually make you negate your own personal needs. This can make you feel depressed and resentful.

- Also, you do not have to feel responsible for the deeds of others. Moreover, when you keep on caring too much for someone and don't let them take any responsibilities in life because you think you can do it all, you are actually hindering their sense of responsibility and ability to think about their own well-being.

You can also attend yoga sessions or hit the gym as it will help in proper energy flow and keep you happy.

Learn to Set Healthy Boundaries

Empaths often forget that they are entitled to set boundaries just like everyone else. If you are not aware of the concept of setting boundaries, then you might think that it is meant to restrict your freedom, but in reality, it is quite the opposite that happens. Boundaries are meant to help you realize your true self and feel your innate beauty and peace of mind. In short, setting personal boundaries means that you are honoring your self-respect and you have clarity on what is yours and what belongs to the other person. It is all about owning your inner space. It will give you the choice of whether or not you want to give someone something. Once you know how to set boundaries, you will also gain control over a lot of things in your life.

The first step towards setting healthy boundaries is being aware of your current situation in life and observing your day-to-day activities. When you attain self-awareness, you will also become more careful about the role of boundaries in your life. Thus, identifying the situations where you need boundaries will also become clear to you.

As an empath, you might be quite habituated to the idea of letting other's energies into your sense of self. But that is not something you should do. You should remember that you always have a choice and you don't have to take on the burden of others. When you do not assert your boundaries, it becomes easier for others to hijack your emotions. When you analyze situations, you will notice that there will always be some people or some moments in which you feel comfortable and safe, and on the contrary, there will also be moments when you feel unsafe. So, you need to create boundaries so that you do not have to face those uncomfortable situations forcefully. When you create boundaries, you prevent yourself from getting totally consumed into the other person. No matter how deeply you connect with them, you never lose the connection to your own self.

Let It Go

Letting go can be one of the most difficult things to do for an empath. When someone is in a state of joy or excitement, it is truly fun to celebrate with them. It can be a new baby or even a job promotion. You feel good when you share such feelings. But on the contrary, when someone is sad or in agony, that is not so beautiful to share. And empaths can even experience feelings of hopelessness. So, if you think that you are experiencing emotions that are overwhelming and draining your energy, then you have to understand that it is your cue to let it go.

When I am telling you to let them go, I am not asking to break all bonds with them. Empaths have the nature of embracing other people's problems as their own. All I am asking you is to let go of that person's emotions and feelings. Loving someone and caring for them doesn't mean you have to embrace everything of theirs as their own. If you are finding it difficult to do on your own, you can find someone who will understand your situation and help you take off some of that emotional junk you are carrying for such a long time. You can also engage in some practice that helps you soothe your mind.

Understand Your Own Emotions

As I have already told you before, empaths tend to neglect their own feelings and emotional needs while attending to others'. With time, they become an expert at numbing their own heartaches and sadness while pouring their every ounce of effort for others. But it is important that you learn to process your own feelings and understand them. Sometimes you might be looking for answers in your outside environment when the answer is right there inside you. All you have to do is take out some time and find those answers. And do you know what the primary vehicle to those answers is? It is your own emotions. Once you embrace them, they will guide you to your innermost self and also help you gain wisdom.

You also have to remember that empaths have the habit of carrying around the emotions of everyone around them and not just their own. That is why it is all the more essential that you start processing your emotions. This is because it will help you distinguish between what is yours and what is not. Your subconscious will no longer be crowded, and you will see things more clearly.

Just because everyone comes to you for emotional support doesn't mean you do not need it yourself. You deserve the same thing when you feel overwhelmed and so you need to make it a regular practice to process your emotions. You can ask a trusted friend to meet you regularly and don't just think about it, fix a coffee date and attend it. If your spouse happens to be someone you trust deeply, then you can also speak out your heart to them before going to bed so that you do not carry the burden to the next day. Or, you can also opt for hiring a life coach or maybe attend group counseling sessions which prove to be very effective. Otherwise, if you are not willing to speak to any physical person, you can also journal every day before going to bed.

Celebrate and Give Yourself a Pat on the Back

Since empaths feel every emotion very deeply, they are aware of both extreme joy and intense sadness, but it is usually the latter that sticks. In fact, empaths cannot let go of the bad things. So, you need to celebrate every joy in your life and feel happy. You need to maintain your emotional balance because continually carrying the negative feelings of others will slowly make you forget what it feels like to celebrate life. For example, you can throw an impromptu part with some of your close friends and family.

Or, you can even spend more time with your kids, read them a storybook, take them to a theme park or gift them something they wanted for a long time. Doing such small acts of kindness will make you happy. You should also go out on self-dates from time to time because they are highly important, and there is no better way of showing self-love than that.

Apart from all the points discussed in this chapter, you also have to take sufficient rest. This will help you relieve the stress that you are carrying the entire day. The first step to take is to ensure that your regular sleep cycle is healthy, that is, you get 7-8 hours of sleep and you go to sleep at a fixed time. You should also practice deep breathing exercises throughout the day, which will ensure your peace of body and mind. You should also avoid overly stimulating situations on a daily basis. Sometimes, it can become unavoidable but you should do your best to be mentally and emotionally prepared.

In today's world, social media can be a highly stimulating environment for empaths, and if you are a social media addict, then I would advise you to go for detox from time you time. Also, you can download apps that prevent you from surfing social media beyond a certain period of time in a day and this will help you practice restraint.

Chapter 3: Love and Sex – A Special Discussion for Empaths

As you already know, empaths feel the world more intensely than the others, and when it comes to love (which in itself is a very intense feeling), everything gets even more magnified. Empaths literally wear their hearts at their sleeves and they feel very deeply. But this habit of feeling everything intensely can also be a bane in intimate relationships because then they have to learn how to set healthy boundaries which are something they clearly don't know. But on the other hand, it is necessary because otherwise, the empath would become overloaded with more emotions than they can handle.

But also, when an empath is in the right kind of relationship where their emotions are values and where their partner understands them completely, then they feel empowered, and it also makes them feel more grounded. But when you are together for a long time, intimacy also has the power of suffocating empaths and so you have to make sure that doesn't happen to you. Since empaths are very sensitive beings, they have this habit of absorbing all the emotions of their partner and making it their own. That sometimes can make them feel unsafe although, on the other hand, even empaths seek companionship. So, do you see how conflicting it can get? Empaths want to be loved and needed just like they do with others but they do not want to get burdened by the needs and emotions of other people. But running away from such situations and seeking shelter by completely isolating yourself from the world is not the solution. The solution lies in protecting your sensitivities by learning how to navigate the world of love and sex as an empath.

Tips to Find the Right Soulmate For Empaths

Empaths become stronger when they feel that they are valued. But in order to make togetherness a bit easier, I am going to discuss different types of emotional people who can be better for an empath as a partner. Basically, it depends on the needs and temperament of the person but this list is going to make things a bit easier for you –

- **Intellectuals** – These people are bright individuals and are also incisive analysts. They have highly rational thinking, and they use it to filter the world around them. No matter how heated the situation is, intellectuals always know how to keep their cool. Whenever it comes to something playful or light-hearted, they might even hesitate a bit before engaging with it. Empaths tend to be more sensual whereas intellectuals will most likely be prone towards staying inside their heads. They are a very big fan of solving problems and fixing situations. You as an empath should tell your intellectual partner about your needs of having some me time, and then you both can together figure out solutions and creative ways in which you can strike a balance in your relationship.

- **Empaths** – Yes, empaths can definitely be with empaths. They both are highly sensitive but loving at the same time. All you have to do is learn how to be supportive and honor the sensitivities you both face. But look on the bright side – you both are easily able to understand things, and so you can easily understand what the other person is feeling. However, the challenge will be in determining your needs and keep it separate from that of your partner's. You need to learn to set boundaries. If both of you become overwhelmed with each other, there can be a lot of anxiety in your home. So, figure out how you both can have some alone time. In the long-term, it is often seen that two empaths can really make a relationship work like no other.

- **Rocks** – These are those people who are stable and have a strong personality. You will not face any hesitation while expressing your emotions in front of these people. They will never judge you or upset you. But the problem with these personalities is that they themselves are not able to express their feelings easily. But rocks and empaths together can make a wonderful couple. They can help each other grow by balancing each other. The empath can teach the rock how they can practice compassion and also express emotions more clearly. Rocks need just a little bit of nudge, and then they will be able to express whatever it is that is going on in their mind. But remember, you, as an empath, will have to initiate things and don't rush anything. Express one feeling every day.

- **Gushers** – These people are the ones who love to express their feelings, and they can also get over negative feelings very quickly. But you must be wondering what their downside is. Well, they tend to share more than necessary and this can lead to burnout in those who are listening. That is why when they are with an empath, they can make the empath feel overloaded. That is why both of you will have to learn emotional sharing.

Tips to Make Relationships Work For You

When you are an empath, then you keep absorbing other people's emotions and that alone can be so exhausting that you might not want to be in a relationship with someone else. This is even truer in the case of live-in relationships where the empath has to share the other person's companionship at all times. This can lead to the development of unstable emotions and a balance between relationships and life, in general, can become quite difficult. But there are ways in which you can make it work for you and here, I am going to give you some tips that you can apply in your day-to-day life as an empath –

- **Always find time to meditate and decompress** – An empath needs to engage in self-preservation on a regular basis, and that can be done by finding some time out of your daily schedule and keep it reserved only for yourself. You can also practice keeping certain short breaks throughout the day. If you are amidst a lot of work, you might tend to forget about the break so make sure you incorporate it in your daily calendar or you can also set reminders on your phone. You should also talk about this with your partner and tell them how important it is for you to have some time alone with yourself. During this break, you will be able to think deeply about the issues that are bothering you or maybe some relationship problems that you are facing. This will also assist you in understanding your partner in a better way. If you think that your partner will not understand your idea of alone time, then you are wrong. You simply have to make them understand lovingly and this will prevent them from feeling rejected. It is true that any relationship would require several compromises to be made but that doesn't mean you will compromise your soul and your feelings in that process.

- **Make changes in your physical space** – The physical state around an empath can impact them in great ways and alter their energy levels. That is why you should be having certain ground rules with your partner about what makes you comfortable and what doesn't. You need to figure out the system that is the best for both of you. It can be something as simple as having a separate nook in the house where you can sit alone and read books or do whatever you want, or it can also be something like using different bathrooms. The adjustment can be anything and usually varies from one empath to the other. You can also make similar adjustments for those times when you are traveling together because you don't want emotional overloads in vacations, right? If you are an empath who is sensitive to smell, then you need to have a look at your chemical sensitivities too and arrange your surroundings accordingly. But whatever it is, if you do not come out with your preferences and tell your partner what you need, they will never be able to understand you. For example, if you are sensitive to any particular perfume or essential oil, you need to insist on not using them (at least not in front of you).

- **Figure out how much you want to socialize** – As I already mentioned in a previous discussion that empaths love to stay alone, or they are sort of introverts. That is why they feel overwhelmed in social gatherings. So, if you are in a relationship, you also need to sort out how much time you actually want to spend socializing. For example, not every empath likes crowded cruises; some simply love a casual day by the pool.

- **You can consider sleeping in different rooms or beds** – Most of us sleep alone while we are growing up, and then suddenly when you are in a relationship, you are expected to share a bed. Some people might love it while others might not and there is nothing wrong with that. So, if you, as an empath, want to sleep in a separate bed, your partner should be able to honor your decision. Or, you can also sleep together three days a week and on the remaining four, you can choose to sleep alone. Empaths also get easily disturbed by snores or any other noises during sleeping and it is also one of the reasons why they prefer sleeping alone.

- **Stop taking things personally** – Maintain the harmony in your relationships by not taking things personally because not every time are the comments personal. You need to learn how to be less reactive.

- **Don't try to always fix your partner** – You need to understand that your partner is completely fine and does not need any type of fixing. Your partner might not always love to take instructions from you on any matter. They also have their personal opinion, and you should be able to respect that. You need to let him/her face their difficulties in their own way.

- **Focus on one issue at a time** – Your relationship might be facing several issues at the moment but you need to promise yourself and focus on only one at a time; otherwise, you will get stimulated. Don't repeat issues. Try to communicate your problems as clearly as possible, and then when you are done, stop overdoing it by reiterating the same thing.

- **Decide on your bath time** – This can seem funny and irrelevant now but this is so important for empaths. They usually love long and uninterrupted warm showers. So, if your bath time coincides with that of your partner, then you need to settle it with him/her. Or, suppose you love to take a long bath before going to sleep, but your partner wants you in bed by them at that time, then that is also something you need to resolve.

Are You a Sexual Empath?

Since empaths can feel everything so intensely, even during lovemaking, they can easily feel and absorb the other person's energies. Sexual empaths have stronger abilities to sense other's emotions than a normal empath and that is why it is also advised that sexual empaths should choose their partners wisely and only then will they get the same amount of respect and love reciprocated.

But when a sexual empath is without a partner for a long time, they jump at the first chance they get and enter into a relationship with literally anyone who sparks their sexuality. They become eager about developing sexual connections that they forget about all other intuitive signs that show the person is not actually the right fit for them from the emotional point of view. They start thinking that they finally got to engage in a sexual relationship with someone who interests them and so the red flags should not matter. But that is also how they make themselves prone to get hurt. They start building an attachment with those who cannot love them back with the same intensity or cannot handle their complex personality.

Chapter 4: Spiritual Hypersensitivity and Its Relationship to Empathy

Hypersensitivity, as a result of spiritual reasons, is commonly seen in empaths. As a result of this, you will find empaths becoming overwhelmed at the most commonplace of things. They can even get irritated with normal range sounds, let alone high-pitched ones, and they can constantly feel what the other person is feeling as if it was happening to them. But this problem can become worse when the empaths deliberately choose to overlook their gifts and not tend to them. One of the very common symptoms noticed in empaths especially those who are on their journey towards greater levels of spiritual development, is that they become extremely sensitive to noise and other people's energy than they were before. It is as if all their emotions are in a heightened state.

Yes, there are certain physical symptoms of spiritual hypersensitivity as well the most common ones being third eye dizziness and, as already mentioned before, sensitivity to things like noise or odor.

Ways In Which You Can Cope With Spiritual Hypersensitivity

You will find that your breathing becomes shallow and the flight or fight syndrome gets triggered whenever you overburden yourself with several mental, emotions or physical tasks that are way too much than you can possibly carry. That is when you should start taking steps towards bringing your spiritual hypersensitivity under control. Here are some things that might help –

- **Move away from the source** – When you have already identified the source which is causing hypersensitivity, then you have already taken the first step. The next thing that you have to do is moving away from that source. First, start by moving away by 20 feet or so and then see the difference. Do you feel any sense of relief? You should not be bothering about whom you have angered in the process of doing this because this is your life, and you have a complete right to do all that you need to do to ensure your emotional welfare. If you are in a public place or a gathering and you cannot stand the energy emanated from a particular person, then try not to sit or stand beside them. You don't have to be rude about it. Just move away politely. Empathy is enhanced by physical closeness.
- **Try Guerilla meditation** – This is one of the best exercises you can practice to cope with spiritual hypersensitivity. Before you go into any gathering, it is important that you center yourself. So, meditation is necessary because it will help you to be strong and feel your heart. In case you come face to face with physical

distress or any form of emotional distress, then you should take some time out and meditate for a few minutes. If you are thinking how, then simply find an empty room and in case you cannot do that, then go to the bathroom and meditate. In case it is a public bathroom, close the stall. You need to calm yourself down and then meditate. Try bringing all your focus on the love and positivity around you. Once you start practicing this, you will notice how relieved you will feel in social functions or gatherings.

- **Concentrate on your breathing** – Sometimes, when there is no way in which you can go to an empty place, and you still got affected by the negative energy in your room, then put all your concentration on your breathing. Do this for a few minutes. This process actually works because you are keeping all your negativity inside the moment you decide to keep your breath in. That is why, when you exhale; you are actually exhaling all the stress, pain and fear and all that you are left with is calmness and peace. It is somewhat like a fog lifting from the valley giving a clear image of what is present. Also, it brings very quick results.

- **Start building healthy boundaries** – Just like in personal relationships, boundaries are necessary in general as well. You need to limit your time and exposure to people who bring about stress in your life. That is why you need to be clear about your boundaries.

Learn to say no. You don't have to be mean or anything. Develop polite strategies of your own and understand the fact that 'no' is in itself a complete sentence.

- **Practice visualizing protection** – Visualization can no doubt be an effective technique to cope with your spiritual hypersensitivity, especially when you use it to imagine that your surroundings are safe and you are protected. It is one of the best healing techniques at your disposal. In some cases, this process is advised to patients too just so that they can feel relaxed and not panic around. All you have to do is visualize that your body is surrounded by an aura of white light which acts as a shield or protective cover for you. There is another way to do this. If you are with someone or some people who are extremely toxic to you, then you can use your imagination and picture a jaguar or any such fierce animal moving around you or patrolling for you.

- **Learn to honor your empathic needs** – This is probably the most important step of all. If you do not respect and honor your needs as an empath, you will never be able to get a hold on yourself. You need to learn how you can safeguard your sensitivities. Once you do that, you can come up with a plan that will help you handle them in the best way possible so that when the moment comes, you do not fumble. Some of these examples should make it even clearer for you –

- If your limit for socializing is two hours, then no matter how much you love the people in the gathering, you need to be out of that place within two hours.
- If someone asks you to do or say something you don't want to, you can simply say 'no.' You are under no obligation to give an explanation for rejecting the proposal.

What Are Some of the Spiritual Healing Tools Helpful for Spiritual Hypersensitivity?

In this section, we are going to talk about the different spiritual tools that you can use to bring your spiritual hypersensitivity under control –

Prayer

The first tool in this list is definitely prayer because no matter which faith you believe, irrespective of that, prayer can always bring you solace and peace from the sufferings you are going through. It can help you wade your way through an overwhelming situation.

And since we are discussing this, there is something that you need to know about as it is quite effective, and it is called – H'oponopono. The main theme of this practice is based on the concept that an individual is responsible for creating his/her own environment and not someone else. It also says that your surroundings cannot be influenced by external forces. The bottom line of this practice is that you are the master of this world, and it should be you who must take the responsibility to care for it. But at the same time, the practice does not encourage taking the blame for the problems around you. What is means is that if you want to make the situation better, you have to start by healing yourself.

Some people do not believe in this theory, but if you think carefully, you might find some practicality in it. For example, if you are someone who always thinks that nothing good is going to happen in your life and that everything is pointless, then you are automatically searching for negativity and putting all your focus on it. But you will see that there is good when you change your perspective. It is just like the concept of seeing the glass half full rather than half empty. You will often find that two people may be in the same predicament but their views, on the other hand, can be completely different.

The concept of H'oponopono has four different steps which I am going to explain here –

- **Repent** – The first step is all about saying, 'I am sorry.' This is where you have to realize that whatever is going on in your mind is your responsibility and not anyone else's. The moment you come to the realization, saying sorry should come naturally to you. If there are things in your environment that are problematic or evil, you have to analyze them and be sorry about the part you played in it to occur. Now, since you are an empath, this exercise should not be that hard as you can already feel others' pain but you have to feel sorry for it too. And you also have to mean it.

- **Ask forgiveness** – Now, when you have figured out that you have made a mistake, it is time that you ask for forgiveness too. You might also be wondering about whom to ask. Well, there is no fixed rule about this. What is important is that you need to ask for forgiveness. Empaths, in general, believe in the presence of higher power, and if you are a believer too then, you can definitely as them for forgiveness.

- **Practice gratitude** – This is where you have to say, 'thank you.' Here too, it doesn't matter whom you are thanking. All you have to do is set all the negatives in your life aside for a moment and then you will be able to see how much positivity your life has. You will come across so many things that you have and you should be grateful for them. You should say thank you that you had a roof over your head when you woke up and you had a wholesome breakfast. You should be happy that you have legs to walk and eyes to see. You should be happy that you have clothes on your body. It can be anything for you, and the list can be endless.

- **Love** – Love is definitely the strongest emotion in this entire universe and in the last step, you have to say 'I Love You.' You need to say it repeatedly until your life is filled with love. You can say it to anyone you like. You can say it to your family members, friends, neighbor or even your pet.

So, this was the practice in a nutshell, and I am sure that you are going to feel so much better if you start practicing it.

Water

There are so many healing and balancing properties that water has, and these become even more profound for a person who is suffering from hypersensitivity. There are so many ways in which you can use it. One such way is pouring a drop of water in the area of the third eye and it will automatically make you feel more energized. Another way in which water can cleanse your body of all the negative energies that have accumulated throughout the day is by taking a hot shower. You will literally be able to envision the negativity from your body being sucked out and going down the gutter.

Mindfulness

Mindfulness is of great help in all situations, and this is definitely true for empaths. You have to get an object on which you can put all your focus and then you can think about something that makes you feel at peace. You have to start by redirecting all your concentration onto some visual that makes you feel happy.

Essential Oils

This is something widely used around the world irrespective of whether you are an empath or not. You need to choose the right blend of oils that are suitable for you, and then you have to massage them daily. You can choose bergamot, frankincense, and lavender. This can not only give you relief from pain but also show a considerable reduction in depression levels. Here are some of the essential oils that are widely used by empaths to get relief from anxiety –

- **Lavender** – It has profound effects on the nervous system and can instantly calm you down. It will make you feel relaxed and also helps in getting better sleep. Some other benefits include relief from panic attacks, restlessness at nights or throughout the day, and relief from stress. There have been several studies on lavender oil, all of which concluded that it could help you in great lengths to give relief from anxiety.

- **Vetiver** – This is one of the essential oils that make you feel grounded and also give you reassurance. If you have experienced some form of trauma recently and it has been troubling you, then vetiver oil can have a calming effect on your nervous system.

- **Rose** – Anxiety, depression, panic, and shock attacks can be reduced to a great extent with the help of rose oil.

- **Ylang Ylang** – The effect of this oil on the human body is highly uplifting, and it not only makes you cheerful but also gives you courage. If you are suffering from insomnia, then too ylang ylang can be one of the best cures. It also helps in soothing fear and heart agitation.

- **Chamomile** – There is a reason why doctors advise you to have chamomile tea at night, and this is because of its anti-depressant properties and also its ability to bring about inner peace. It can also give you relief from general irritability and eliminate the symptoms related to anxiety.

- **Bergamot** – If you are fond of Earl Grey tea, then you must know that bergamot is one of its constituents. It helps relieve insomnia and agitation. It can also reduce pulse rate and blood pressure.

- **Frankincense** – This oil too, has been found to be used when it comes to depression and anxiety.

Now, you must be thinking about how you can use these oils. Well, one of the ways in which you can use them is through aromatherapy. The limbic system is a particular area of your brain that gets triggered through strong responses as in this one and recalls past memories. Thus, a mental response is stimulated whenever you inhale an essential oil. This also leads to the lowering of blood pressure, change in breathing patterns, or the production of certain hormones in your body. So, you can use a few drops of these oils in a humidifier, hot water for bathing or even inhale them directly.

There are a lot of oils which can be consumed orally as well. But you need to be sure about the purity of oils as a majority of them in today's world are synthesized. One of the most common ways in which you can consume them orally is by mixing them with honey. You need only a drop of the oil. Or, you can even take two drops of the oil of your choice and place it beneath your tongue. This method paves the way for quicker absorption of the oil. Some of the essentials oils are also available in the form of capsules in the market.

Then, there are some oils that can be used topically. You can use them on your teeth, nails, or even hair and skin. But since the oils can be very strong, it is advised that you make them dilute before applying them directly. The dilution should be done with some type of carrier oil like jojoba, avocado, or coconut. Then, you can apply the mixture. You can apply it on your scalp, your feet or even with the help of a warm compress.

Chapter 5: Energy Vampires and How Empaths Can Protect Themselves?

Energy vampires and narcissists are attracted to the empaths. It is very similar to how a flame attracts the moths. And every empath is bound to have one or more energy vampires in their life. It could be your friend, your spouse, your parent, or even a colleague at the office. They can be shaming you for possibly everything like your body size, your income, your social status and so on and soon you will be drained of all your energy. When matters become worse, the insults can take the form of abuse as well.

Being with an energy vampire is like walking on eggshells. This is because they can get irritated very easily and make themselves distant, and empaths keep admiring and praising them just because they do not want to hurt anyone and keep the peace. But that is how your self-esteem takes the blow and you might start to feel that the problem is not with them but with you.

Also, when such endless insults are hurled at a person, the level of cortisol in your blood starts rising, and this has other implications too. You might give in to alcohol or other forms of substance abuse or maybe start making poor dietary choices. In most cases, empaths do not identify energy vampires in their life and when they do, half of their energy has already been sucked out.

Now, if you are wondering how an energy vampire can affect, I have jotted down some of the ways in which you can be affected by an energy vampire –

- When you are around an energy vampire, it is as if someone has poured tar on you, and now it weighs you down. You can feel completely immobilized and you can even have some physical symptoms of it like sweating of palms and heart beating faster. The levels of hopelessness start rising and the energy vampire keeps showing too much toxic entitlement. They have this complete disregard for other people's emotions which can drain an empath completely of all their energy. With all this going on around you, it will be very difficult to concentrate on those things which really matter to you in the long run. Energy vampires keep using several manipulative tactics so that you put all your energy in serving their ego and not for your own good.
- When you are with an energy vampire, you get used to the habit of ruminating, and so you keep feeling emotionally exhausted over things that happened in the past. There is always a persistent self-doubt looming over your head and you keep questioning the existence of your own identity. Depression and anxiety are

sometimes inevitable in empaths who have been impacted by an energy vampire.

- The moment you step away from energy vampires even if it is for a span of a few days, you will feel lighter and better. You will gain better clarity on life, and you will feel as if someone has lifted some heavy weight off your shoulders. But when an empath goes back to interacting with those energy vampires, they fall into the same cycle of emotional exhaustion once again.

- Energy vampires have this tendency to make you feel confused and disoriented, even when you are discussing something quite simple. You will find yourself explaining the same things again and again about fairness and basic human decency. You deserve a certain respect in your life and you will often find that energy vampires deny giving you that. When you try to talk about their behavior, they might even try to project on you the toxic traits they possess.

- Energy vampires have a parasitic nature. They will literally leave you malnourished in terms of energy. They will always try to undermine you or sabotage you whenever you are happy or joyful or confident.

- Reciprocity is an alien concept to energy vampires. They always want the other person to keep giving them and fulfilling all their needs. Everything is one-sided. Even when you are in a conversation with them, you will notice that they keep talking about themselves and not anything else. In order to feel powerful, they always try to micromanage.

- As far as the narcissistic spectrum is concerned, energy vampires are quite high on that and so they have feelings of jealousy and envy when you are doing good in life. They do not celebrate others' successes because they want what others have and when they cannot have it, they try to sabotage that success. They are also skilled in plotting plans to demean others.

So, if you think you have experienced all of this with a person, then he/she is the energy vampire of your life, and you need to cut off that toxicity and negativity from your life as soon as you can. Here are some of the steps that you can take.

Refrain From Giving Too Much

Since empaths have this natural tendency to be compassionate to everyone that comes their way, they are often at risk of giving too much to energy vampires, which they clearly don't deserve. So, if you think that you are feeling depressed, stressed, irritated, or exhausted when someone is present around you, then you need to take a step back. It is true that personal evolution, spiritual growth, and psychic awareness are all enhanced when you give but you also need to strike a balance. You cannot keep giving endlessly; otherwise, it is going to hamper your health. There must be equal amounts of receiving and giving.

The first step is to identify what intention the other person has. Finding out the intention is an essential step towards judging whether the relationship is healthy or not. Then, start weighing up the situation. If you arrive at the conclusion that the relationship you are in is nothing but valueless, then you need to stand up and step away. You should not let someone else leech away your emotional energy. There may be times when someone gave you a compliment, and you felt good but that doesn't mean you always have to reciprocate with another compliment. You can also say thank you and move on.

Don't Get Into People-Pleasing

People often give in to people-pleasing because they think that will make other people like them. But that also makes you vulnerable to the energy vampires. Also, sometimes the habit of people-pleasing takes the form of a behavioral pattern that is toxic. You should never think that people-pleasing is just another form of kindness because it is not. It is nice when you try to be kind to people and do something for them. But it is not right when you always keep going out of your way to help someone because that is when you are compromising your own needs.

If you are a people pleaser then

- you will often find yourself in situations where you are not able to say no,

- when you get hurt by someone, you cannot express your feelings,
- you always seek validation otherwise you cannot feel good, and
- whenever someone is upset or angry with you, you feel overwhelmed.

If you want to break free from the cycle of people-pleasing, then you have to accept the fact first. Sometimes, when you try to people please anyone and everyone you meet, you are your own energy vampire.

Learn Efficient Time Management

Now, you might be wondering where time management comes into play when you are thinking about ways to get rid of energy vampires. Well, it does. If you want to protect yourself from the energy vampires, then you should also focus a bit on spending time with the right people and by this, I mean your friends and family who make you happy. Think about it this way – you already have a busy schedule; so, is it worth it to be with someone who leaves you emotionally exhausted even after a 5 minutes conversation? The answer will be no.

You need to assess your energy limits, and you need to respect them. You cannot force everything on yourself and still expect to do just fine in your life because that is not possible. So, you need to set aside time from your daily schedule during which you will spend some time with yourself and also with those who love you.

Ground Yourself

Grounding yourself is so important when you are dealing with energy vampires in your life. If you do not know what this means, then let me give you an intro. You have to promise yourself that you will not be swayed by any form of negativity that is around you. Being affected by an energy vampire is very similar to getting sucked into quicksand, and if you are successful in grounding yourself, then you will become resistant to such things.

In order to that, you can practice meditation or even mindfulness. Do whatever works for you but make sure you are completely grounded as far as your energy levels are concerned before you interact with any energy vampire. You need to think of yourself as an old tree whose roots have gone deep into the ground, and no storm can uproot you.

Be Careful About Choosing Your Battles

Energy vampires are usually those who have rigid beliefs, and arguing with them will drain all your positivity. It will not only cost you all your energy but also your precious time and you cannot afford to do that. Yes, it can be tempting to argue it out or disagree with someone but you should also understand the fact that you cannot really change someone if they themselves are not willing to do that. If someone is refusing to understand your point of view and continuously going on about how wrong you are, then there is no use getting all red-faced with them. You are upsetting yourself and getting stressed just for nothing. It can even affect your health badly. So, you need to be careful while you choose your battles.

Listen To Your Body

Your body has its own way of telling you things through various signs and physical symptoms, but you have to keep an eye out for that. When you have interacted with an energy vampire, you will find that your body is trying to tell you that you are exhausted in some way or the other. You might feel fatigued or experience a headache. So, if you want to fight off energy vampires, you need to start educating yourself about the signs that you might experience when you come face to face with them. You simply have to listen to what your body is trying to tell you.

Try to be in a Group When You Are With an Energy Vampire

If you have to interact with the energy vampire at all costs, then you can do so by staying in a group. Even if you have a couple of friends or colleagues with you, it should be enough. When you are talking with an energy vampire on a one-to-one basis, then all that negative talk is hurled directly at you and not anyone else. But the energy vampire will have to divide his/her attention to multiple people when you approach them in groups. So, you can steer clear of the pessimism exuded by that person and being in groups will minimize the effect.

Also, if your friends are good at dealing with an energy vampire, then there is a lot that you can learn from them as well. You will be able to observe how they are talking with the energy vampire.

Stick to Topics That Are Light-Hearted

If you are talking with an energy vampire, try to keep the conversation focused on topics that are light-hearted and not too serious. There are certain energy vampires who are easily triggered by topics that are too close to their hearts. When the negativity surrounding a particular topic is too deeply rooted in the conscience of the energy vampire, you have nothing to do about it, and so the best way would be to change the topic of the conversation. You can lighten the mood by speaking about what books you read, what movies you watched or even the weather in general. You can even talk about your common friends. Your aim should be to neutralize the conversation by sticking to mood-uplifting topics.

Stay Calm

This is another very important strategy for you when you converse with energy vampires. Since energy vampires feed on other people's energy, they are literally waiting for you to react and get agitated and so you should try to do the opposite. The more you react and show that the conversation is bothering you, it will encourage the energy vampires even more. You cannot give in to the bait.

In case you think that you cannot take all this negativity anymore, you can always leave the conversation and there is no harm in that. There will be some days in your life when all of this leech-y behavior can seem frustrating. So, you need to take a deep breath and walk out of the conversation. You can go and spend some 'me time' if that is what helps you, but you can also go and spend your time with people who make you happy.

Never Feel Guilty

As empaths are emotional sponges, they are very easy targets for the energy vampires, and it goes on like a vicious cycle. When they cut them off from their lives, empaths feel guilty as they are too emotional and feel that it is their responsibility to understand what everyone feels. But you should not consider yourself just because you set some boundaries. Setting boundaries is essential. It does not make you a bad person. You should put your mental health and yourself above everything else in life. So, when you take the decision to set some boundaries, there is nothing wrong with that.

Energy vampires can make you feel bad about yourself and drain your energy even in a small and brief encounter. So, you need to be very much careful and identify the energy vampires in your life at once. When you are armed with knowledge, you will be in a better position to use these strategies. Also, you need to know that it is not your responsibility to answer every question the energy vampire asks you. In fact, when you do so, you are actually giving them more power over you. So, what you have to do is be clear about what makes you uncomfortable. If you are not willing to answer something, then don't. Don't give in.

But if none of the strategies mentioned above are working in your favor, then you have to understand that it is time for you to cut off that person completely from your life or at least start limiting contact. In case that person is in your team and you are co-workers, then you can limit your contact only to those issues which are related to your work.

Chapter 6: How to Build Connections With Others?

When you start becoming aware of what you want and how you can do it as an empath, that is your first step towards a change. It can be mind-boggling sometimes but when you have complete knowledge about your situation, things will automatically start becoming easier. Have you noticed children when they fail to make you understand what they are feeling? They start fussing or crying but when they find the right way to express their feelings, they can easily calm down. The same thing happens with empaths as well. When you learn to build connections and convey your emotions, everything becomes easier and sorted in life.

If you want to bring about any changes in your life, you need to start by accepting your qualities as an empath. You also need to accept the entire situation that you are in. You need to see yourself as someone worthy of love and attention, and you definitely do not have to be so hard on yourself. Empaths often fear that they might end up being egoistical and that acts as a barrier not only in forming connections but also in self-love. You need to build a healthy regard for yourself and that is not something selfish.

For empaths, the world is hard to describe, and so are their feelings. They do not have faith in their perceptions or their validity. But when they start to get a grip on why they feel or do what they do, that is when all the chaos starts to smoothen out. They can understand situations now because they have identified the patterns or structures that are there. But for that, empaths first need to learn how they can build the connections with others without hurting themselves and for that, I am compiled some useful tips for you.

Understand Energy Exchange

There are several ways in which you can understand and measure energy. Now, you have to understand that one of the most vital things that keeps you alive is energy, and it can be felt in various ways. Your emotions or feelings are one way of measuring your energy. If you are an empath, you will know how exhausting it can feel after you have had conversations with a certain person. These people are toxic for you and automatically drain the energy out of you (as discussed in the previous chapter). Even when you do not talk much, you can get exhausted simply by staying in the presence of such people.

On the contrary, you will also have people in your life who make you feel comfortable, and you will feel happy around them. This person can be your friend or even a family member. But what you have to understand that empaths always undergo these energy exchanges whenever they communicate with someone.

You absorb the energy of other people and you let them do the same to you subconsciously. What you need to do is understand that you have your own aura. It is somewhat like your own personal bubble which determines your energy limits. All your emotions and thoughts are present in your aura. All your traumas are present there too.

So, when you connect with someone, you are taking in the energy that is present in their aura, and you are sharing your aura with theirs. This energetic field exchange does not always happen through talking. Sometimes, you can experience the same with a total stranger who is sitting next to you on the train.

Learn to Create Barriers

This is so important when it comes to effective communication. Empaths are so affected by what other people feel that they often mix up all the emotions and then confused about their own feelings. They cannot separate others' feelings from their own. That is why it is so necessary to create barriers so that you learn to ground yourself. If an event or a person has bogged you down, it is in your hands to stop it, and you can do so by creating a barrier. The simplest method is to avoid people or locations that give you that feeling but as you know, it is not always possible to avoid. Sometimes, you have to interact with people you don't want to and so that is when you have to make yourself strong. You can try to meditate or practice mindfulness to create strong barriers in your mind.

Use visualization to distract your mind from the negativity and tell yourself that what you are feeling is not yours. It is someone else's emotion that you have absorbed. You need to let that toxicity go because only then will you be able to see your true self.

Another way of creating barriers is by saying the right things. But this will take some time, and you have to work on increasing your levels of self-confidence. For example, if you are in the middle of a conversation with someone and you do not like where it is headed, then you can always ask them politely to change the topic because you do not feel so good about it. Or, you can excuse yourself from the conversation and take a break. You need to prevent yourself from getting drained of all the energy you have and you need to do everything you can to keep yourself stable – that should be your ultimate goal.

Challenge Yourself

If you want to communicate better, you need to go out of your comfort zone. Communication is the key in all aspects of today's world, and if you keep yourself shut down, it is not going to do you any good. So, you have to learn to open up. Most empaths are introverts and opening up can be a big challenge for them. That is why, introvert or not; I always advise empaths to do something that is new to them because it will give you the lesson of handling anything that comes your way. You need to understand that there is room for improvement in everyone but change or improvement will only come when you take the first step. Here are some things that you can do to challenge yourself

- **Learn a new language** – One of the best ways of challenging yourself is by learning a new language. Also, it won't go waste is you choose the language to suit your resume, and then you can even earn some extra cash on the side. This is not even difficult as you got plenty of apps providing free resources and also amazing YouTube videos where you can get language tutorials.

- **Pursue a hobby** – Everyone has something that they always wanted to do but couldn't because they did not get enough time. So, figure out what your hobby is and then pursue it. You can monetize this too once you learn it well.

- **Do something you are scared of** – Think about what scared you. Are you afraid of public speaking or maybe heights? Then, take a small step towards your fear, and once you do that, you can take another step towards it next week. Yes, the first try can be scary but don't leave it at that. You should look at your fear in the eyes and face it.

- **Travel** – When you travel, you meet new people from various cultures, and this will eventually help you in sharpening your communications skills as an empath. You will meet people outside your usual circle and you will come to realize that everyone is different.

Practice Active Listening

Empaths are good listeners and that is why people come to them during their sorrows. But if you want to form better connections with people, you still need to brush up on your skills. Being an empath means you are absorbing other people's energy right from the morning. If someone impacts you too deeply, you might be thinking about that particular situation the whole day, and so when you try to communicate with the next person, you are not really listening as your mind has been diverted towards the previous person.

Also, not all empaths are active listeners. Some empaths listen for a while, and they wait to respond. You should be really listening to the person until the very end. Your body language also plays a big role in making the person in front of you realize that you are actually listening to them and not pretending to do so. Always maintain eye contact. Keep responding to them in full sentences. Simply saying single words like 'absolutely' and 'yeah' doesn't really count. You should come up with full sentences that have your judgment in them.

Engage in Self-Love

If you want to enhance your communication skills, you also have to work on loving yourself. You show empathy to others, and you are kind to them. Now, you have to practice some self-empathy. One of the ways in which you can do this is by trying to talk to yourself just like you do with those you love. Empaths have this habit of beating themselves up for every little thing but talking to yourself like a friend might help you in solving this problem. Take a piece of paper and write down any negative thoughts that you are having about yourself and then tell yourself the positive things that you would have told a friend experiencing the same thing in their life.

You can also get rid of the endless cycle of self-judgment by practicing mindfulness. Think about your feelings and emotions, but you should not be judging them. Just let them come into your mind and then let them go as if they are free-flowing. Don't ruminate on anything and at the same time, don't push any of the thoughts away.

You should be able to forgive yourself. You need to remind yourself that you did what you could with what you had at that moment. Everything that happened has also given you some good lessons in life. But I am not asking you to shield your wrongs or pretend that they did not happen. What I am asking you is to accept that you made a mistake and then forgive yourself for it. Once you do this, you are practicing self-compassion. This means that you have learned to identify your own humanity.

Also, you need to stop comparing yourself with others. This is the era of social media where people are constantly checking through others' profiles and then comparing their life with theirs. But whatever you see on social media is just a photo. You do not know what is going on behind that. So, if you think that social media is making you upset, you need to reduce your time scrolling through the various social media accounts.

If you follow all these steps, you will soon be proud of yourself the way you are, and then you will not feel shaky or tense when it comes to speaking with other people. If you want to thrive as an empath, self-love is the key to it.

Prevent Nervous System Overdrive

Since empaths are so vulnerable to negative energies or anything that can make them upset, they often experience nervous system overdrives. And when this happens, it can numb your ability to communicate or connect with someone or interact with them in a proper way. Sometimes, the overdrive can become so serious that empaths experience occasional burnouts, depression, and anxiety attacks. But if you want to prevent all of this from happening, you first have to work on preventing this overdrive from happening.

For that, you need to balance your nervous system and your energy levels. Your nervous system, as an empath, catches the energy from different people throughout the day. It might start by catching a smile from your kid in the morning and then move on to a very sad friend you met on the bus and then the meaningless complaints of your boss at the office. So, there is a constant shuffle between all these emotions. In between processing all this information, your nervous system can easily run into overdrive. This results in chronic stress, as well.

So, you need to learn to identify the signs of an overdrive way before it happens. If you sense anything like increased heart rates, sweating, agitation or headaches, then you need to take a break no matter what. You can go to an empty room and simply focus on your breathing. Take deep breaths. After a moment, you will notice that your heart rate has returned back to normal, and consequently, so has your nervous system. You should also try out restorative yoga.

Fear and anxiety are two of the most common emotions that will be provoked in your time and again because of your nature of being too sensitive as an empath. And this can bring you tons of miserable experience over the years but you need to relax. You need to remind yourself that your life is a journey and there will be ups and downs. You need to put your best foot forward and the rest will unfold slowly.

If something needs to be addressed now, don't keep it buried or don't procrastinate about it. Your life is already unpredictable, and you need to be okay with that uncertainty. You have to understand that you cannot predict everything, even though you are an empath. Empaths who have the habit of neglecting their gifts are the ones who suffer the most. When you repress your qualities, that is exactly when your energy levels are going to become even more unbalanced than ever. You need to be more proactive and you need to embrace yourself for the person you are.

There will be times when you will be so exhausted that it is almost discouraging, but you cannot give in. Otherwise, you will have to start over once again. If you want to interact with people in a better way, you need to navigate your energy levels using multiple strategies. You need to neutralize every situation that comes your way and you need to turn every negative into a positive. The best way to thrive as an empath is to create a balance and embrace your emotional, physical, and spiritual being with open arms. Analyze your current situation and take some time to do that. Jot down what needs to be balanced and the work on one situation at a time.

Chapter 7: A Step-By-Step Approach to Building Your Emotional Intelligence

When it comes to improving your relationships, EI or emotional intelligence is a special skill that you need to acquire. It will assist you in managing your own emotions and also understand others better than before. Also, according to various types of research done in this field, it does not matter what your academic aptitude is. You can still start brushing up your emotional intelligence. The four skills which form the core of emotional intelligence are as follows –

- Self-management
- Self-awareness
- Relationship management
- Social awareness

If you are wondering why you need to acquire emotional intelligence, here are the reasons –

- The success you acquire in your life is not actually proportionate to the amount of education you received but to your levels of emotional intelligence.
- The various social complexities that come in your path right from your childhood to your workplace can be

navigated smoothly once you master the art of emotional intelligence.

- It will also help you acquire the necessary leadership qualities. You will be getting a great outcome from your subordinates at work, and you will also be able to motivate others.

- No matter how difficult the situation is, emotional intelligence will help you understand it.

- Your physical well-being is also benefitted from emotional intelligence. This is because it helps you achieve a balanced emotional state where you do not have fluctuations in your blood pressure or your heart rate.

- You will be able to combat depression and anxiety and ensure mental peace.

In short, if you want your life to go on smoothly and harmoniously, then acquiring emotional intelligence skills is highly necessary.

Step 1 – Reflect On Your Emotions and Label Them

You need to take some time out from your daily schedule and sit down with a piece of paper for this exercise. Think about all those times when you asked someone about something (suppose, how their week was), and the answer you got was 'fine.' Isn't that vague and unsatisfactory? The same applies to you. Emotional literacy is something that needs to be taught but is often neglected in everyone. Very few people in this world know how to explain their emotions accurately. And, when it comes to empaths, they are even more confused because of all those emotions they have absorbed from others and they have now compiled into one.

There are so many nuanced emotions you experience throughout the day, and then there are those emotions that have quite a greater intensity. Some emotions may be complex while some simple and yet you fail to produce the right word for it. For example, rage and agitation are not the same things but different levels of anger. So, if you want to avoid any form of miscommunication, the first thing you need to learn is the art of emotional labeling.

If you want your own emotional well-being, then it is necessary for you to start working on emotional labeling right away because it will help you to rightfully express your inner experience. Also, the faster you are able to express what you really feel, the sooner you will be able to resolve so many conflicts in your life. Your emotions have so many intricacies and without the right vocabulary, it is impossible to find the right word. For example, at first, you might feel that you are simply angry at a person but if you probe deeper, you might realize that anger is only the upper layer. What you are really experiencing is betrayal, and anger is just a way of showing the actual emotion lying underneath.

When you are able to articulate your feelings in the right manner, you will be able to get the upper hand even in the most difficult conversations. You will be surprised to know that the words available to describe your feelings fall in an endless list. But people are so used to putting the general words in everything that they do not bother about knowing what else is out there. You need to look up from the primary feelings and research the secondary feelings as well. For example, sadness can be diversified into melancholy, self-pity, sorrow, grief, and so on. Similarly, enjoyment can branch out to satisfaction, pride, relief, joy, and so on. If you want to climb the ladder of emotional intelligence, labeling your emotions in the right way is definitely the first step.

Step 2 – Ask Others For Their Point of View

Now, understanding your own emotions was all about becoming mindful and aware, but you also need to understand that the same situation has different perspectives, and you need to know about them to get a clearer picture. There is a myriad of factors that influence the perspective of a human being. It can be their friend circle, their upbringing and the list goes on. And all of it happens subconsciously. But the problem is we often forget the fact that our perspective might not match that of the person in front of you.

Don't get me wrong. There is nothing called a right or wrong perspective. It is simply different for different people and these differences have their own consequences too. So, when you interact with someone, whether it is your work colleague, your close friend, or someone from your family, you need to ask them what their perspective of you was. For example, if you had an emotional outburst in the morning, you can go to them later on and ask them how they would describe your behavior to be. You should also ask them to explain the same situation by relating to something similar they had gone through in their life. If the situation involved you, then you should also ask them how you dealt with them at that time and were you sensitive or not.

Once you do this exercise, you will understand how others see you in different situations and also how assist you in understand the perspectives of others in a better way. Then there is another thing that you need to be aware of, and it is called perspective gap and practicing to understand others' perspectives will help you bridge this gap. But first, you must understand what it means. When you are not in an intense state of physical or psychological nature, then you have the tendency to underestimate the effect of that situation on you. An example should make this clearer. There are pieces of evidence that show that when patients are in pain, physicians usually underestimate the pain because they themselves are not facing the pain. So, they fail to understand how much the intensity of the pain is. That is why inspiring empathy by following the techniques of emotional intelligence is so important as it will help you understand others better and bridge the perspective gap.

Step 3 – Be Observant

Now that you have learned two important steps of developing emotional intelligence, you have some newfound knowledge in your lap and if you utilize it properly, then you will be able to be more observant of your emotions and feelings. Very few people in the world are observant, and it is a trait that comes from natural human instinct. There are ways in which you can improve it and these are as follows –

- If you want to accept the difference between things, then you need to start by accepting the differences. If you are not interested in the things around you, then it is not possible for you to become observant. You have become a great observer when you learn to spot the differences between you and others, and once you do that, you should start asking questions about the existence of that difference.

- The next thing that you can do is become self-aware. Every action that you take or word that comes out of your mouth has consequences, and if you do not understand these consequences, you will never be able to understand what is truly going on. When a person is self-aware, they are mostly at ease with everything and display a calm demeanor. They always work on their insecurities and try improving them. The more you work towards becoming self-aware, the more observant you will become.

- If you want to be observant, you have to look for the visual cues in your surroundings. No matter how much information you get from spoken or written things, visual things will always provide you with more knowledge.

- You need to keep asking the 'why' questions more. It's like creating a loop for yourself where your brain will be hungry all the time. In this way, you will learn to become actively involved with your environment.

- Another important thing is to learn to read body language. No matter how much you talk with a person, the majority of conversation is actually non-verbal, and people often fail to notice that.

When you combine the knowledge you gained from others about their perspectives with that of your self-reflection, you are already one step ahead in the learning process. You will automatically be in better tune with your feelings. But in case you come across some new things and experiences, you need to reflect on your feelings and label them, and for that, you have to go back to step 1.

Step 4 – Express Your Emotions Assertively

When you master the nondestructive way of expressing your feelings, thoughts, emotions, and beliefs, that is known as assertive communication, and it is one of the core skills that you have to learn if you want to master emotional intelligence. When you are expressing your views, you need to be frank and forthright about them. But people often tend to mix up aggression and assertiveness whereas both of these are two complete opposites. When you act in a hostile manner that is called aggressiveness but when you argue constructively and stand up for what is right, that is when you engage in assertive communication.

You might hear it a thousand times that you have to be yourself and authentic if you want to move forward in life. But it is not just about wearing your emotions on your sleeve. There is so much more to it that you are not aware of. So, in order to make things a bit easier for you, I have spoken about five of the most common emotions and how you can express them with the help of assertive communication.

- **Vulnerability** – Expressing your vulnerability is definitely important, but you also have to understand that there is a difference between undermining yourself and sharing your insecurities. For example, suppose you got a great gig where you have to speak publicly and you tell your friend that public speaking has never been easy for you then it is the right way of expressing your vulnerability. But instead of saying that if you get up on the stage and say something like you are not comfortable in speaking in front of everyone, then that will definitely undermine your abilities and also lower your audience's expectations.

- **Joy** – Joy is an amazing emotion, and it has the ability to cultivate so much dedication and a sense of purpose, but only when it is communicated in the right way. Let me give you a workplace example. Suppose you want a productive atmosphere in your office and in order to culminate that, you give free goodies to your employees. But that can backfire as some extrovert employees can involve in exuberant activity and this, in turn, can cause a distraction among those dedicated employees who are actually trying to get things done. So, instead of doing that, you can give them a motivational speech and also tell them how excited you are about the work that you all are doing as a team.

- **Anger** – Anger is definitely one of the trickiest emotions to communicate. Conflict, frustration, and anxiety are some of the things that cause anger. But if you want to be emotionally intelligent in such a situation, you have to take a step back and analyze your anger. You have to think about whether it is really necessary for you to show that kind of intense feeling. You can achieve clarity in such situations if you identify what is the cause of your frustration and then move as far as possible from that cause. Now, focus on expressing your feelings in a way that is not aggressive or hurtful. You need to shove past the problem and focus on the solution. Pay careful attention to the words you use, and there should be no accusatory tone. You need to remind yourself that venting is never a helpful thing to do.

- **Empathy** – As an empath, you will understand the feelings of everyone around you, but sometimes, there are chances that you might end up going overboard with it. It is good to empathize with people but it not good or even right to let the toxicity of someone else ruin your life. You need to understand their point of view but at the same time, you need to build the resistance that you will not be affected or influenced by their emotions.

- **Fear** – This is another emotion that you will have to come face-to-face in your day-to-day life. If you think carefully, you will find many such situations where you were tongue-tied. But if you want to approach this situation, you first have to accept the fact that you get anxious at times. Never try to suppress your emotions; otherwise, they will keep building up and your fear of certain things will also start escalating.

Step 5 – Respond, Not React

Passive-aggressiveness or explosive anger is not the right way to answer. If you do that, then you are being shortsighted and impulsive and you cannot afford to behave that way. These situations arise when you have some unresolved issue or you are not getting what you planned for or what you wanted. But instead of reacting to the incident, if you learn to respond, then you are bound to get better results. You will be able to assess the situation and get a perspective on how you should react. You will also be able to find the best approach to handle things in a better way.

You need to assess the situation as a whole and not stick to any single part of it. You need to tap into the feelings of everyone involved and get everyone's perspective. Also, before you act in any manner, you should solicit the opinions of others too. If you want to become emotionally intelligent, then you have to learn to see beyond the drama and recognize the facts for what they are and not how they are presented to you. You will be required to put on your calm demeanor while diffusing a difficult situation. This will go a long way in helping you to come with a solution that not only satisfies everyone's demands but also is constructive in nature. You have to be open-minded while accepting other people's opinions on the matter.

It is true that feelings of anger and emotional outbursts are very common when you are in the middle of a conflict, but you cannot afford to get carried away. The moment you make any decision based on your impulses, that is when you are paving the way for bigger problems. Your only goal should be thriving for a proper resolution and not breathing life into the conflict. Also, you need to be conscious about your choice of words and make sure that they are in line with what you are actually trying to communicate.

Step 6 – Be Self-Motivated

One of the personal skills that you need to acquire in order to become emotionally intelligent is self-motivation. This means that if you want to achieve something in life, you should have the personal drive to do so. You should be fully committed to your dreams and practice resilience and optimism. Every person is different when it comes to self-motivation. What motivates you may not motivate someone else.

You have to consider your mindset if you are going to work on increasing your self-motivation. People usually have two types of mindsets – the growth mindset and the fixed mindset. Those who have a growth mindset use their skills along with effort and hard work to improve in life. But those who have a fixed mindset are the ones who stay boxed up and believe that their ability cannot be changed as it is ingrained.

When your general well-being is considered, goal setting is extremely important. You cannot achieve something in life if you do not have your aim at it. Also, moving forward is only possible when your aim is set at something. After that, planning the path to get there will become easier.

After that, you have to learn to take full advantage of opportunities when they come your way. When you hesitate to do that, the opportunity will not keep standing at your door. It will go away. But before you take any initiative, you also have to think about risk management. This will help you to choose the right opportunities so that you take only that much risk which you can afford to take. Also, you must gather up your courage because when you are taking something new, there will always be the fear of the unknown, and you have to fight it off.

Then comes your task of building your resilience. You should also look on the bright side. No matter how great the setback was, you should have the strength to bounce back. Sometimes all those overwhelming negative thoughts that you are having can blind you, and you fail to see that they are not at all logical. But when you practice logical thinking, you will be able to overcome the effect of such emotions.

Your motivators can be both extrinsic and intrinsic, or it can also be a feeling of obligation that drives you. It is your sense of duty and responsibility that gives rise to the feeling of obligation and it can be quite a strong feeling to keep you going. You do not have to work on all of this at once. Start with one skill at a time and soon you will have mastered them all.

Step 7 – Always Keep a Positive Attitude

Your attitude determines a lot of things, and you should not be underestimating it at all costs. When you become emotionally intelligent, you will be able to shield yourself from the fluctuating moods of those that are present around you and this is all the more important for empaths who have the habit of absorbing other people's energies. It can be a daily challenge to maintain a positive outlook at all times but you have to try your best to do it.

The main obstacle in your way is the fact that our brains have been designed to always look for threats in the surroundings. And the same mechanism gives birth to negativity, pessimistic attitude, and sometimes even egoism. If you want to stay positive, it has to be intentional; otherwise, it is not possible. You need to stop your negative self-talk right now and that is the first step towards maintaining a positive attitude in life. Getting out of your self-defeating vicious cycle of thoughts can definitely be difficult but once you do so, you will see the world in a different light. You need to do what you need to maintain an optimistic outlook. This means that you can also practice meditation or do some physical workout as it often helps in eliminating negative energy from your body.

Chapter 8: Self-Confidence and Self-Esteem – Two Things That Empaths Should Work Upon

Empaths are often found to struggle with self-confidence and self-esteem. They have a very low sense of worth. They rate themselves really low. And when these two qualities are present in low amounts, the empaths lose their balance. As you know, empaths are healers, and they expend their energy, trying to make others feel better. They forego the foundation of their own lives and do not take care of their own selves. Instead, they spend all their time and energy in assisting others. That is why they have low self-esteem and self-confidence in the first place.

The low levels of both these qualities are usually deeply rooted in the past and mostly in the childhood years of the person. It can be some form of trauma or emotional abuse. It can also be something like constant neglect from a parent, separation from parent figures, and sexual abuse. When you have low levels of self-esteem, you start seeing the world as this bad place where nothing good is possible. You automatically see everything in a hostile manner. And this is very commonly seen in empaths. This is also the reason why they miss out on so many interesting things in life, and they also feel that they cannot change things because they have become powerless. And this goes on and on like a vicious cycle lowering their self-esteem even further.

But if you want to break free from this downward spiral, then there is definitely a way out. There are several strategies that you can implement to enhance your self-confidence and boost your self-esteem. Here are some of them –

Practice Visualization

Visualization can help you in many ways when it comes to empowering yourself. In this technique, you have to see yourself as the person you want to be or the person you are proud of. This is because when people have low self-confidence, it is because they view themselves in a poor perception. This perception is not always accurate. But when you visualize yourself as the person you are trying to be, then you get an immediate bout of self-confidence. It might seem a bit daunting in the beginning, but with time, you will be able to improve your self-image.

You have to implement the strategies of creative visualization to achieve the results you want. It will identify all the negative beliefs that you have about yourself and then replace the same with positive ones. Yes, it will not happen in the span of a night, but you have to take the first step towards it and stay consistent if you want your efforts to bring fruitful results. Your aim should be protecting your subconscious from the negative thoughts and you also have to work on eliminating the toxic thoughts that are already present there.

So, your first task is to find a place where you can perform visualization. The place should be quiet and safe, and no one should disturb you there. You have to choose the place in such a way that you can be there for a period of time totally uninterrupted. You can also play some music that is relaxing or light some candles to create a soothing atmosphere. Then practice deep breathing for a few minutes as it will help you in eliminating the stress from your body. After that, close your eyes and start visualizing. You have to imagine yourself as this strong personality who does not get affected by petty negative matters in life. Your imagination cannot be vague; otherwise, it will not take effect. You have to be very specific about all the details you see.

No matter how busy you are, you should try to take out time on a daily basis and practice this exercise. If you can, then you can also do this twice a day for better results. You have to encourage yourself with motivational words and praise yourself. But you also have to remain patient. Remember that your negative self-image was not born in a day. It took you years to become like that, and so it is definitely going to take some time to undo that damage.

Create Positive Affirmations

When you utilize daily positive affirmations, it can really change the way you see your life. Affirmations are like these small positive statements that can keep you focused even when you are not, and they will help you overcome anything that comes your way.

Create your own positive affirmations that you will repeat throughout the day and keep them written in someplace and go through it right after you wake up in the morning. This will set you off in a good mood, and you will have the right vibe of energy in the morning. You have to believe in yourself that you can do it; otherwise, nothing is going to be possible.

Now, if you are wondering how you can create positive affirmations, here are some tips that you should keep in mind –

- Always use first-person because that gives a certain empathic feel. Say 'I am' instead of anything else. This will sound really powerful.
- You should always stay in the present tense while creating your affirmations.
- You have to make it specific. You cannot be vague as to 'I will try to eliminate self-doubt.' You can say, 'I will not second guess my abilities in public speaking.'

- You should keep these sentences in the positive. You have to affirm that you want something. The sentences should not be about what you don't want.

- Try to include the –ing words because they indicate action.

- Keep them concise and short. When you have a lesser number of words, your affirmations automatically become easier to recall. You can also try rhyming them.

- You should center these affirmations around yourself. They should not be about someone else in your life.

- There must be a 'feeling' word or some kind of dynamic emotion in your affirmation.

Once you have written down your affirmations, you have to make a promise to yourself that you are going to repeat them every day for at least five to ten minutes. I would always advise you to say them out loud because that exudes a high level of enthusiasm and energy.

Face Your Fears

If you want to increase your self-confidence levels, then you will have to come out of your comfort zone and face your fears. You have to remind yourself that self-confidence is nothing but a mindset that you have to acquire. Yes, you will feel powerless when you are afraid, but you also have to remember that you can take over your fears. Start by writing down your fears. Take a notebook and think about all those things that make you feel afraid. Once you have written them all down, now it is time to rank them according to the anxiety levels they cause.

Now, after you have ranked them, start from the bottom (the one that is least-anxiety inducing) and face them. You have to slowly work your way up the list. The first one that you try should not be too hard, and once you do it, you will automatically feel a boost in your self-confidence. Eventually, you will come to those fears which are of most importance in nature.

It is also important that you start rewarding yourself for every fear you face. This is because when you reward yourself, you automatically start attaching the feeling of overcoming fear with good feelings. The reward does not have to be anything elaborate. It can be something as simple as treating yourself to your favorite food, or it can also be watching your favorite TV series for a while. But one of the most important things about facing your fears is that you have to be honest with yourself. If you are not honest, then there will always be some fears that will stay suppressed. When you start meeting your fears head-on, every experience will give you newfound confidence.

Keep a Check on Your Inner Critic

Empaths often have an overactive inner critic and that is why they keep criticizing themselves more than necessary. If you think carefully, then you will notice that the harshest comment your receive on anything are usually from your own self. This not only lowers your confidence but also affects your self-esteem.

People are often so used to hearing their narrations that they do not really judge the messages that we are sending across to our subconscious. We tend to become oblivious to everything. You have to pay careful attention to whatever your thoughts are, and you need to remind yourself that not everything you think is true. Some thoughts can be biased and exaggerated.

You should also stop ruminating. Suppose you had a bad day at the office, and you kept rethinking all those moments over and over again which eventually led you to have a bad day at home too. When you keep on repeating the bad things in your head, you are actually making yourself feel worse. Also, there is a tendency in people that they start focusing on the same matter they are trying to avoid. So, the more you try to avoid something, the more you will be attracted to it. The solution lies in finding an alternative thought that you can stick to and this thought should be something positive.

You also have to learn when your thoughts are becoming too negative. In order to do so, gather all the evidence that you have in your possession and then examine them one by one. You will notice that the evidence will ultimately refute the prediction that you have made. If you are finding it difficult to gather the evidence to support your thoughts, writing them down in a piece of paper often helps. You have to be rational while you judge both sides of the argument.

Slowly, you have to learn to accept your flaws. Nobody is perfect, but instead of reminding yourself that you are not good at something, you can also try to encourage yourself to do better. When you accept your flaws or your weaknesses, it does not mean that they have to remain the way they are forever. You can always make progress if you want to.

Your inner critic has both positive and negative effects. It can either help you in achieving your full potential or it can completely ruin your chance of success. When you are too harsh on yourself with the self-talk, you are hindering your pace and reducing your chance to achieve your goals. So, when you tame your inner critic, it will help you know which areas require improvement, and then you can start on a more productive journey.

Stop Comparing Yourself to Others

Empaths have an identity that is very much vulnerable to the outside world, especially because of the fact that their self-esteem is not in good shape. They get easily affected by the energies of those around them. Whenever they are in some social gathering, they start comparing themselves to others.

They start judging themselves on the basis that they are not good at something while others are. It can be the simplest thing in life but it can also be something complex.

But you have to realize the fact that you always try to focus on what you lack and not on what you have. When you continue to do this for an extended period of time, your brain becomes wired to disregard your own feelings and strengths. You take on a lot of stress than you can handle, and your performance is heavily affected because of this. What you have to do is learn to appreciate the skills that others possess. You need to stop seeing everyone in a way as if they are your competitors. Instead, you need to learn things from them by considering it as an opportunity to brush up on your skills. Your demeanor will undergo a lot of change the moment you change your perspective.

The human brain is meant to learn a lot of things when you do something on repeat, and that is why if you want this strategy to help you, you have to practice not comparing yourself to others whenever you are in a social place. When you keep doing this over and over again, it will become your second nature.

Stop Worrying About What Others Think

Empaths have this tendency to judge themselves based on what other people say or think. Their actions become totally biased. They cannot determine their personal value and always depend on others to do that for them. Also, in today's society with so much social media presence, it is pretty easy to get caught up with your outer appearance. So, you need to strengthen your thoughts and stop worrying. The social norms are the major reason why people worry about other people's perceptions of them. There is always something that is considered to be ideal, and whenever you deflect from the idealism, you start questioning yourself whether it is right or not. You fear that others will reject you or judge you. But you have to remind yourself that there is nothing wrong with you. The society has simply grown like this and it is responsible for inculcating this fear of judgment in everyone.

You have to learn to live in the moment and not worry about anything else. When you keep worrying about the smallest things in life, you lose confidence in your own self and suffer from low self-esteem. You cannot control everything in your life and so stop trying. Focus on who you are and ditch all the 'could' and 'if's because they are not your problem to worry about.

There is something else that you should consider. If you think carefully, you will notice how much we all are centered among ourselves and so is everyone around us. We might be thinking that others are constantly judging us or discussing something bad about us but that is not the case. People don't even care usually as they are concerned about their own problems just like you. Suppose when you are going out on a date, you might be thinking what others will think of your outfit but chances are that no matter what you wear, it will be the same to most people. Once you start to realize this, it will become easier.

Practice acceptance. You need to everything else at the bottom of your priority list and put yourself on top. You should be your biggest priority, and you should practice giving self-love at all times. You will learn about the various ways in which you can show self-love in a later part in this book. It will take you some time to get used to all of this but with a little bit of practice, everything shall fall in place.

Be around those who make you happy. You need to choose your friends carefully. Don't be with people who criticize you or make you feel bad about yourself. When someone truly cares about you, they will focus on your strengths and remind you what a good person you are. Also, when you feel judged, it really helps when you are in your group of friends, where you can discuss everything openly.

You also have to make yourself understand that no matter how hard you try, there will always be people in your life whom you cannot satisfy. No matter what you do, some people will always judge because that's the only thing they know. But those people should not really matter to you. Our life is too short to worry about such things and waste half of it. So, ditch all negative thoughts and enjoy your life to the fullest.

Chapter 9: Empaths, Intuitions, and Extraordinary Perceptions

Empathy and intuition are two completely different abilities within a person. Generally, an empath can feel and sense the energy and emotions of other people and his or her surroundings. Empathy is nearly about facing outward completely and relating to other things rather than oneself. On the other hand, intuition influences you to turn inwards and discuss your insensible mind and gut feeling to evaluate and analyze a situation. It depends on processing the environment around an empath. But empaths are known to have excellent intuitive powers too.

Signs That You Are an Intuitive Empath

There are some significant signs which are present in a person that shows that you are indeed an intuitive empath.

- **Ability to explain the comparison of feelings between yourself and other people:** An empath can absorb the energy and feeling of other people within their mind. As a result of this, he or she may feel disturbed because they have absorbed all the negative energy, and now they cannot separate it from their own feelings. For example, empaths become anxious when they take anxiety from other people. But an intuitive empath can keep their feelings and emotions separate without any impact on their mental status when they accept their surrounding environment or other people's emotions within their mind.

- **Ability to find out the reasons behind feelings:** Empathy paves the way for you to embody others' feelings as if it were your own. Non-intuitive empaths become confused when it comes to detecting the reason accurately behind their feelings, and they can't explain the reason properly. But intuitive empaths have a wide range of perspectives to visualize anything. It helps them to find out the link between reason and impact of anything. They have a greater insight into every emotion and they can immediately understand why a person is feeling a certain way.

- **Both an advisor and a counselor:** If you can feel another person's emotion and also have the power of visualization, these qualities may help you to act both as an advisor as well as a counselor. Generally, intuitive empaths have the power of creativity, and they can think of every situation in different ways. It helps them to get the solution to any kind of issue efficiently and easily. If anyone has failed to figure out a solution for any issue, intuitive empaths can readily find out the correct and effective solution which is important to the other person.

- **Supportive for other people and realize their mental status:** Intuitive empaths support people to help them realize their mental status. Specifically, they like to talk to people and they become completely involved in their thoughts, satisfaction, dreams, emotions, and worries. They can easily grasp the feeling of others and even understand those things which the other person is not able to frame in words. These qualities help them to understand the detailed picture of others' feelings and thinking patterns. It also helps them to identify the potential and the actual reason behind their feelings. Intuitive empaths are always helpful to others. They can analyze any kind of circumstance and also other's mental conditions. Moreover, they can provide the right advice with proper explanations stating the advantages and disadvantages of the solutions related to the particular situation.

Types of Intuitive Empaths

1. **Dream Empaths:** People can dream in a natural way within their sleep, and they usually forget the dream when they wake up. But dream empaths are different as they can remember their dreams in detail. They frequently visualize the situation and signs of their surrounding environment in their dream. It helps them to understand the actual scenarios regarding real life. If you are a dream empath, you can experience vivid dreams regularly. It will help you to get intuitive

information clearly as the dream is a type of strong intuition. It is an advantageous way to find out the solutions for difficult situations, get knowledge about the guideline regarding spirituality, healing, and the defeat of various emotions.

As a dream empath, you can easily move in different matters during your dream time. You can improve the ability to remember your dream and acquiring knowledge from a dream. It helps you to understand yourself and others efficiently. Moreover, you can interpret the dream by understanding the meaning of some symbolic things which come in your dreams. These symbolic things are water, color, people, and numbers.

2. **Telepathic Empaths:** They apply their ability for intuition to read the events which are occurring with another person in their presence. Telepathic empaths can guess the unexplained feelings and think of another person. They can receive intuition from various directions such as their friends, family members, co-workers, and even strangers present within their surrounding areas. Telepathy is a type of connection that is made without considering the sender's or receiver's will. Telepathy helps to make mind-to-mind communication of feelings, concepts, and thoughts. Telepathic empaths can develop a relationship to a great

extent. If you are a telepathic empath, you can even communicate with animals telepathically and can understand them easily. The practice of telepathy techniques requires a great extent of patience, mind power, focused concentration, and strong beliefs. A calm state of mind is very important when you apply telepathy techniques. Mind training is also an important factor for being a telepathic empath.

3. **Earth Empaths:** They can make bonding easily with natural elements. Earth empaths can energetically and sensually feel the beauty of the moon, the strength of a thunderstorm, and the warmth of sunshine. They are affected greatly due to seasonal changes. If you are an earth empath, you can feel any change on earth. You may feel anxious, affected, and even get health issues if there cause any harmful effects on earth. As you are more sensitive to earth than any other people on the earth, you may be happy due to the happiness of the earth or maybe sad due to the bad condition of the earth. If you want to increase the power of making a connection to the earth, you will have to practice it frequently. Spending more time within the natural environment can help you to develop sensations to the earth. You can travel to places with mountains, forests, oceans, and seas to spend your time within the natural environment. You may feel sad due to any kind of natural disaster such as earthquake, flood or tsunami hits as you are an earth empath. You

can be sensitive to the occurrence of any change on earth such as weather change, changes in high tide and low tide, and also astrological changes.

4. **Precognitive Empaths:** They have premonitions regarding the future when they are in their dream or in their awakening condition. You can develop your skill for premonition by practicing the power of premonition frequently. Precognitive empaths can receive premonitions regarding several things, such as someone's relationship, health, career, and any kind of issue in life. A clear concept for using foreknowledge including integrity, is essential for a precognitive empath. As a precognitive empath, you can help others by giving a warning for the upcoming dangerous or stressful conditions in life. A precognitive empath can know the event in advance before they occur. You can experience foreboding sensation before the happening of something bad for being a precognitive empath. You can provide the right guideline to the people for making decisions regarding any matter or for avoiding potential disasters. You can achieve the power of premonitions through physical sensations, emotion, and vivid dreams.

5. **Mediumship Empaths:** These are those empaths who have the special ability to get in touch with spirits, animals, and even people who are present on the other side. They can navigate the great divide that is present in between, and they join the gap that is present between

your afterlife and present life. They believe in the existence of something beyond the material plane. They are an expert in receiving an intuitive message by setting their intellectual minds aside for a while. If you are an empath who falls in this category, then you should try to advance your skills under a mentor. Mediumship empaths have this ability to console those who are in grief. But no every person who claims to be a mediumship empath is authentic. Some of them are shams too. But the authentic ones do exist and they have existed since ancient times. Also, just like any other empath, being a medium can also be burdensome at some times. If you want to keep your qualities in control and your energy grounded, you will have to shield yourself from negative influences. If you think that you are uncomfortable with some experience, then you must remember that you always have the right to say no. You will start to be comfortable with this once you start understanding the fact that mediumship is nothing but just another extension of your empathic abilities.

6. **Animal Empaths:** They have strong sensitivity towards the animals and are able to make a connection with them. If you are an animal empath, you will be able to understand the feeling of animals. You can communicate with them telepathically. You can be more sensitive to caring animals. You may have a strong, energetic feeling and consciousness of the animals like a

veterinarian. An animal empath's exceptional ability to realize and recognize the mental condition and emotion of an animal is advantageous to communicate with animals. It helps you to influence an animal's character positively. Generally, there are many differences in the different animals' characters. If you have enough knowledge regarding animal behavior, it may help you to analyze properly the feelings or emotions of the animals. You can study psychology or biology of animals to develop your power as an animal empath. Moreover, you can choose training courses to work as an animal healer. You can use your special talent as an animal empath to treat issues of animals. Sometimes, animal empaths are vegetarian or vegans, as they are deeply connected to the animals. You can understand the signals and sounds made by the animals as an animal empath. You can try to protect the animals from being mistreated by the people within the society.

7. **Plant Empaths:** They can understand plants' needs properly in different conditions and environments. If you are a plant empath, you can think and understand a specific plant by taking care of it properly. You can strengthen your bond with the plants by studying the plant. You can choose your profession related to plants such as research work on plants, works related to gardening, and so on when you are plant empath. It may be advantageous to fulfill your job satisfaction. You can

feel pain and become sad when any plant is injured or broken. Generally, plant empaths have enough awareness and lots of knowledge regarding the functions and uses of plants. They know which types of plants are poisonous or edible. They also know in what way the plants maintain sustainability and ecological balance within the environment.

Protection Strategies for Intuitive Empaths

The main step to follow the protection strategy for intuitive empaths is to identify instantly the first sign of feeling sensory overload or the starting point of receiving stress or negative energy from others. If you want to maintain balance and protection, this step is essential for being less stimulated and centering yourself. At the beginning of the moment when you are experiencing the feeling of exhaustion or overwhelm, you can follow the protection tips given below.

- **Shielding:** Shielding is an instant way of protecting yourself against negative, harsh, and lower energies. You can compare it with using an umbrella when you are walking in the rain. It ensures the safety of your energy from being polluted or disturbed when you are working or passing through a harsh environment. Visualization helps to connect your thoughts and mind with your brain. You can distract yourself by changing psychic information or pattern of emotional thoughts for shielding. Sometimes, empaths or responsive people block out negative or toxic energy, which may resist the free flow of positive energy. It is important to shield yourself whenever you feel discomfort with a person, situation, or place. You can take a few long and deep breaths. Breathing helps to circulate negativity and then eventually throw it outside of your body. The slow and deep inhalation and exhalation can reduce uncomfortable energy. Otherwise, you can hold your breath or take breathing shallowly to attach to your inner self. You can visualize an exclusive shield of colors with white or pink entirely covering your body and imagine that it is extended to a few inches like an aura. It is an effective protection strategy to resist a toxic, stressful, negative, and intrusive thing. It is also advantageous to feel happy, centered, and energized. There are different types of harsh environments to create toxic, stress, or negative feelings. For example, when you are working in a company that has lots of political gaming, competition, or negativity.

- **Set energetic separators at home and workplace:** The intuitive empaths receive stress from their surroundings using their energy as they are highly sensitive. Sometimes, an excessive stimulating and noisy environment of home or workplace can make them invaded, confused, and angry. They can protect their energy level by using energetic separators. If you are a highly sensitive or intuitive empath, you can keep plants or photos of your family or pet within your space. This method may help you to protect the energy level when you are in a crowded or emotionally demanding environment. You can use sacred objects such as statues of God or Goddess, Buddha, crystals, sacred beads or any kind of protective stone to set energetic boundaries. Noise preventing equipment such as headphones or earbuds are also advantageous to minimize sounds or conversations.

- **Know the definition and explain your relationship requirements:** You can follow a strong form of energy protection strategy by knowing the definition and explaining your relationship for being an intuitive empath. When you feel the presence of any wrong thing within a relationship, you should raise your voice against it instead of suffering silently. Raising your voice can help you to find your power. Otherwise, it may influence you to become anxious, exhausted, or sensitive similar to a doormat but within the relationship. As a result of this, you may be dissatisfied and not be able to meet your basic needs. It is important to maintain safeguards by explaining your relationship requirements. It is also important to think that your partner is not a mind reader. You can ask yourself many questions such as 'Would you like to spend time quiet or alone? Would you like to talk more with your partner? Would you like to enjoy a special day with your partner?' It is essential to reveal true feelings. There is no reason for holding back or being ashamed.

- **Resist empathy overload:** The releasing or minimization of negative energy is very important to resist empathy overload when you are absorbing emotions or stress from your surroundings. You can calm yourself by inhaling essential oil like lavender or using a few drops midways between the space of your eyebrows. Time management is a major factor in maintaining your mental hygienic condition. You can refresh your mind by spending time in nature or within the environment which you like. Some simple strategies may help you to manage your time such as you should not plan for doing several things of your personal life in a single day, or you should learn to cancel plans if you think that you can get overloaded. As an intuitive empath, you should not feel obliged to go outside when you require to rest or you are tired. It is possible to resist an empathetic overload by avoiding toxic people and energy vampires. You can enhance your energy level by practicing self-compassion instead of beating yourself up. For example, you may appreciate yourself at the end of overcoming a hard day.

- **The practice of meditation for jaguar protection:** You can maintain jaguar protection by practicing meditation. It is advantageous to prevent the entering of negative energy. This represents the patient to be fierce to keep away toxic people and negative energy. By following a deep meditation from your heart, you can create a calm environment within your mind for calling a jaguar spirit to ensure your safety. The spirit of this power will take care of your space of energy and save you by keeping out negative energy and intruders. This is an effective way to feel safe within the boundary of the jaguar's security. Your ensured protection and safety will help you to maintain the responsibilities of your own self instead of being victimized by other people.

The highly sensitive people or intuitive empaths must learn the method for dealing with sensory overload after feeling it immediately. The above-mentioned protection strategies are very important to intuitive empaths. All of these strategies can keep them safe from being exhausted, depressed, sick, or anxious. It is essential to understand the condition of overloaded sensitivity at the beginning so that you can take action for remedies to overcome or eliminate this type of situation as soon as possible.

Chapter 10: Self-Care Tips for Empaths at a Glance

As you already know, empaths are very sensitive to the sorrows, pains, and griefs that other people suffer around them. The amount of sensitivity displayed by an empath can even go to such an extent from where they can forego their own needs to meet the needs of those who are suffering. The sensitivity they show might bring a lot of benefits, but giving up on their own needs for others might bring an obsessive behavior over the course of time. Research shows that the habitual denial of own needs might cause obsessive-compulsive disorder (OCD) in which a person subconsciously and recurrently carries out the act. To get rid of such symptoms of OCD, following self-care tips are quite necessary for the empaths.

Carve Out Alone Time

Continuous engagement with others' pain can obsess you badly. A short escape from such engagement can help you to reduce the secretion of stress hormones within your body. So, no matter how busy your schedule is, always try to take some time out for yourself. A 2017 research has shown that only 15 minutes of solitude can refresh your mind. Not only that, but the research also mentioned that if you practice it regularly for at least seven days, the result is just amazing. You will feel much better than earlier. Your body and mind will be more peaceful, calm, and relaxed. But the amount of alone time needed by a person usually differs, and so you need to figure out how much time you need.

Manage Your Time Wisely

Twenty-four hours make a day for everyone, and it is applicable for you too. So, you have to prioritize your daily work schedule to bring a balance between everything including your self-care, family-care, and professional matters. Overcommitment to anything can overwhelm you and cause fatigue and obsession. A better way of prioritizing your daily work schedule can be preparing a to-do list for a day on the preceding night. This will enable you to just focus on the most important work at the top of the to-do list. Once you get the work done, you will feel a tremendous momentum that will promote you to progress onto the next work. In this way, you can utilize your time appropriately and feel the pleasure of satiety.

Practice Self-Compassion

Self-compassion is truly the foundation of self-care. In other words, treating your own self compassionately should be your priority. So, self-care and self-compassion are like putting yourself before anything else, and giving your own needs the upper hand. You have to think that your inner-self is your best friend. Neither you nor anyone else is perfect. So, don't beat yourself up. Treat yourself with all your kindness. You should do at least one act of kindness for yourself every day. For instance, when you accomplish the first job of a day, cheer-up and tell yourself 'good job' or 'excellent performance' or take a short break of ten minutes and walk alone. Practice deep breathing. This habit will boost your spiritual development.

Balance Your Personal and Social Needs

You have to find out the fine line between your own needs and the need for others. The difference can teach you how you can meet the needs of both ends. Sometimes the empaths who are too sensitive can go to any extreme point to meet the needs of other people. Such a situation can overwhelm you, and you can feel lonely or isolated from your inner soul. Such circumstances can make you a slave of your hectic schedule. So before being trapped by a hectic schedule, your situation demands to make sure you are preparing a well-balanced work routine that can fetch you the quality of your own well-being and social life you always wanted.

Listen to Fatigue

The necessity for balancing your to-do list arises when you feel forced and fatigued due to shouldering excessive workload beyond your capacity. The moment you bend down before your work pressure, the obsession begins haunting you. So, before obsession absorbs your whole energy, you should listen to your body and mind and prevent fatigue from consuming your energy. Unless you take adequate rest and adopt quality self-care practices, the delicate functional system of your body will not allow you to restore your energy and thrive in some new work.

Set Healthy Boundaries

A relationship between two persons in all cases can be healthy if there lies a clear thread of boundary between their thoughts and actions. If that fine line of boundary disappears or has been set inappropriately, the relationship does not work well and breaks your soul, placing you in a depressing situation. A distinctly defined behavioral boundary works like a fence or boundary wall, main gate, and the door of your house that protects you from trespassers and mischievous persons. In other words, a healthy behavioral boundary also protects you from the people who want to take advantage or to cause you any harm. Therefore, in order to set a healthy boundary, you need to know your inner self, your likes and dislikes, your comforts and scarcities, and how you deserved to be treated by the other person in a particular situation. So, you need to be very clear and specific while handling other people so that the people can also know their boundaries.

Tune in to Nature

Healthy boundaries that you have set to deal with other people may sometimes not work properly for your self-care. This happens when the need for your self-care does not align with the need for caring for others. If you fall under such a situation, you immediately should get back to the previous position and scrutinize between your thoughts and actions. Always remember that whether your stress level will remain under your belt or gear up depends on your feeling of two factors. The first one is the feeling of love that brings peace, tranquility, and motivation to a positive vibe while dealing with other people. The second one is the feeling of fear that brings uncertainty, anxiety, sadness, loneliness, and anger while you fail to manage other people and their needs. That situation almost burns you out and impacts the social relationship. So, better, you should tune your schedule with time before time burns you out.

Be in the Now

In general, the mind of people randomly shifts from one thought to another in a chain style, which ultimately distracts a person from the initial thought. For example, while dining out with your partner, you might be thinking about what will happen with your money or your business. Such type of mental noting or thinking practice can distract you from the present moment. This symptom deprives you of enjoying the present moment. Under such a circumstance, you can meditate for gaining mindfulness that can bring you back to the present. The mindfulness practice of meditation can help you to live in the present with happiness and peace without agonizing with other unhelpful thoughts.

Create a Life You Love

Usually, people spend a monotonous life every day. They even don't feel many new things coming in the way of their lifestyle. But one thing for sure can be said that the ordinary moments that you spend in your everyday life carries the seed of your future life. So, if you honestly want to build something new in your future life, you should create a life that you love. Creating something new in your future life begins within your brain and mind. At the initial stage of thinking, you might not even know about how to deal with your thoughts and might be not sure about how much time it may require to fulfill your dream. But, one thing is definite that you must have a strong belief to fulfill your dream. In real life, you can make a substantial change with your patience over time and strong commitment towards your goal.

"No" is a Complete Sentence

Self-care necessitates creating a boundary for your own about 'does and don'ts' according to your capacity and capability. Don't-s emphasize on rejecting those issues which are beyond the capability to deal with. For instance, people forcing you to do such a thing that can cause harm to you cannot be acceptable. In that case, you have to say 'No,' and it is not your fault that you want to say no. The single word 'No' describes a complete sentence with full meaning that keeps you free from anxiety. Saying 'No' does not mean you are incapable but it expresses your inner strength to decide about what is just and what is unjust.

Positive Self-Talk

Your energy level depends on your thoughts, and it influences the biochemical reactions within your body. The production of endorphins or "feel-good hormones" in biochemical reaction helps to boost up the positive attitude. It also increases the secretion of stress hormones which are advantageous to deplete the negative attitudes within your body. Your positive attitude results in positive self-talk, an affirmative power. It resists you to focus on negative or fearful thoughts. For example, you may be depressed for the seasonal disorder. But your positive self-talk can help you to overcome your depression. Practicing positive self-talk is a great option to feel easy and natural in any kind of uneasy or unnatural situation or event. Happening of events in your life doesn't depend on your wish. But you can change them by transforming your attitude using positive self-talk.

Attracting Love

Attracting love or feeling love is one of the best tips to take self-care for an empath. You can be careful about your diet and beauty to feel self-love. It is important that you maintain a good appearance, which is essential to get self-confidence and a positive attitude. You can do exercise daily to improve your health or to maintain your body fitness. Good health is advantageous as it keeps your mind fresh. Regular exercising improves the secretion of endorphin hormone which creates happiness within your mind. You can make your dress by choosing your favorite colors and wear your favorite clothes for encouraging self-love. Getting a new haircut is also another way to engage in self-love. You can also come up with new strategies of productivity to focus on improving work performance and that would be an act of self-love too.

Make Time for Silence

Silence or a quiet environment can allow you to gain energy. A noisy environment can drain out your energy. A peaceful and silent atmosphere is advantageous to concentrate your mind. For example, nature stays dormant covering with snow in winter, and this condition of nature can be compared with maintaining silence or a quiet environment to gain energy. The acquired energy of nature is essential for blooming flowers and also to create a beautiful appearance of nature in the springtime. You can practice staying silent or quiet at any place such as your home, office or any outdoor place for a specific time in a day to acquire energy which plays an important role in caring for yourself.

Breath Out Stress

You can feel relaxed by taking long breathes during a stressful day. The breathing involves sacred life energy according to the traditional texts of various religions. When you breathe in, you take oxygen, which is essential to break down food for releasing energy within the body. On the other hand, you breathe out carbon dioxide which not essential for the living body. Similarly, you can breathe in to get oxygen to reduce your stress and breathe out harmful emotions or negative thoughts to maintain self-care. Sometimes, animals hold their breathing or breathe slowly to hide or protect themselves from their predators. Similarly, you can hold your breathing to constrict energy for your protection or self-care as a sensitive person.

Befriend Your Body

If you want to flourish your quality of empathy, befriending your body is very important. Your body acts as a receptor when you receive the emotions of others as an empath. The strength within your body helps to survive with the different types of emotions. Your body allows you to store energy or spirit, which supports you to absorb toxic or negative emotions from your surroundings. You should think of your body as a sacred temple and you should take care of it. The proper care of your body is advantageous for being energized. It will help you to stay alive with a fresh mind by overcoming the ill effects of toxic or negative emotions. For example, you should take a break when you think that you have been overloaded as an empath.

Conclusion

Thank you for making it through to the end of *Empath Survival Guide: A Practical Guide for Highly Sensitive People to Build Connections With Others – A Healing Workbook to Develop Your Emotional Intelligence, Improve Self-Esteem and Self-Confidence*, let's hope it was informative and able to provide you with all of the tools you need to achieve your goals whatever they may be.

I am immensely happy that you have completed this book, which shows that you really want to apply the strategies in your life and let me tell you something – you do have the potential to do so. There are so many empaths in the world and you will realize that it is really a boon to be an empath when you are able to embrace your qualities and use them for the benefit of not only others but also yourself.

You also have to understand that not everyone will have the same experience. Your survival journey might not be similar to your friend's. Your journey should be about self-exploration, and then it will automatically seem to be fun and not forced. You should also understand that the aim of this book is not to encourage changing your empathic nature but to help you in embracing it.

I sincerely hope that all the knowledge that you have gained from this book helps you in challenging your fears and overcoming barriers that come your way but above all, encourages you to engage in self-compassion and self-love. Remember that empaths are incredibly strong, and so you simply need to understand how you can utilize this strength and direct it towards your own success.

Finally, if you found this book useful in any way, a review on Amazon is always appreciated!

Printed by Libri Plureos GmbH in Hamburg,
Germany